THE WORK OF THEOLOGY

By

Francisco P. Muñiz, O. P.

Translated from the Latin
By
John P. Reid, O.P.

𝕸𝖊𝖉𝖎𝖆𝖙𝖗𝖎𝖝 𝕻𝖗𝖊𝖘𝖘

www.mediatrixpress.com

MMXV

ISBN-13: 978-0692464748

TABLE OF CONTENTS

I. THEOLOGY AS A KIND OF POTENTIAL WHOLE

1. THE NATURE OF WHOLE AND PART

*E*VERY science partakes of the nature of a whole which is composed of many parts, for in each science numerous and diverse material objects are presented for consideration, and these must be reduced to the unity of some formal "ratio." Hence the supreme value of considering a science under this formality as a whole. In the doctrine of St. Thomas, three kinds of whole are distinguished: (a) a universal whole, (b) an integral whole, and (c) a *totem potestativum* or potential whole.[1]

We call a universal whole one which enters into each and every one of its parts with its complete nature and with all its power; so, for example, animal is a universal whole in relation to horse and to man, because the entire essence of

1

animality as well as all of its force or perfection are found both in horse and in man. Horse and man are said to be and in fact are subjective parts of animal.

The integral whole is found to occupy the opposite extreme, since it enters into each and every one of its parts, neither in its nature nor in its power, but rather results from all the parts taken together. This is evident in a house or in the human organism, the essence and power of which are merely in actual contact with all of the parts, and not in any one or several parts taken by themselves.

The parts of which this sort of whole is made up and into which it can be divided are themselves called integral.

These are either homogeneous, as the parts of the Mediterranean Sea, or heterogeneous, as is the case in the parts of a house or of a living organism. Heterogeneous integral parts are not all of equal perfection, but some are more and others less perfect. The foot or the arm are not of the same importance in the human organism as the heart or the head.

Between these two types stands the *totum potestativum* or potential whole, which enters into its individual parts with its complete nature—wherein it agrees with the universal whole—but not with its total power—wherein it resembles the integral whole. An example of this sort of whole (the classic example cited by St. Thomas) is the human soul with respect to its vegetative, sensitive, and intellective functions. It is the same human soul and the whole human soul which vegetates, which senses, and which enjoys intellectual knowledge. Thus the 'whole human soul is active in each of its functions. But its complete power is not active in each function, for in the function of vegetating, the sense and intellective powers play no part; and in the function of sensing the vegetative and intellective powers remain inactive, and so on. The complete essence of the soul is found in each and every one of the vital functions taken individually, but the soul's full power is not active except when all the functions are taken together. It is clear from this illustration that a potential whole, from the part of essence, bears a strong and necessary similarity to the universal whole, but on the part of power, it approaches the terms of the integral whole. Therefore, it is properly designated by St. Thomas as a mean between the other two.

All the parts composing a *totum potestativum*—thereby termed "potestative," or potential, parts—are rooted in one and the same nature, e. g. the soul, from which they spring. They all share in the power and perfection of the whole, not equally, but more or less, according to various degrees. This multiplicity of powers and operations or actions results from the greater eminence of the essence, which in its perfection is the equivalent of many essences. Thus, by way of example, the human soul—a single existing form—is able to exercise the operations proper to a vegetative soul, those peculiar to a sensitive soul and, over and above these, the operations proper to it inasmuch as it is rational and intellective. The human soul, one existing form, includes within its power a multiplicity and variety of operations; hence, it is a *totum potestativum* or potential whole.

Since potential parts participate more or less in the power of the whole, they must have among themselves an order and subordination, based on their greater or less participation in the power of the whole. This is apparent in the human soul itself, in which the vegetative acts are essentially subordinated to the operations of sense life, and the complete activity of sense life naturally subserves the operations of rational, intellective life.

2. SCIENCE UNDER THE *Ratio* OF A WHOLE

NOT all sciences partake equally of the nature of a whole. In the first place it must be established that every science is some kind of integral whole. Now this is not to be understood on the part of the habit of science itself, as though this habit were an aggregate of many habits or qualities. In the doctrine of St. Thomas, a habit for its own part is a completely simple quality.[2] The notion of integral whole in sciences it must be insisted: (a) arises either from a greater or less extension of the habit itself to diverse objects or, (b) from the part of the material object, which, since it can be multiplied, establishes a sort of total or adequate object resulting from the union of all the material objects. Like matter, extension cannot but bring about division into quantitative, and thence into integral parts. Thus the metaphysical tracts on substance, quality, causes, God, etc. are integral parts of Metaphysics itself, since this science embraces the consideration of being in its total extent.

Some sciences also take on the nature of a universal whole; these are all those and only those which can be divided into diverse species as Mathematics, which is divided by scholastic philosophers into Arithmetic and Geometry. But those sciences, the formal ratio of which is indivisible and atomic, cannot have subjective parts, nor, consequently, can they take on the nature of a universal whole. Physics and Metaphysics are of this type. That a science may possess the formality of a potential whole, it must, in its own proper nature, contain actually and in a more eminent mode the perfection of several diverse inferior sciences. In the natural order, only Metaphysics enjoys this prerogative, including within its scope, actually and eminently, the perfection of the other, inferior sciences, and indeed the perfection even of the habit of first principles, for Metaphysics is a wisdom which comprises within its extent the perfections both of science and understanding.[3] Hence Metaphysics is at once both an integral and a potential whole. As an integral whole, Metaphysics has various integral parts, which are the different tracts on being, the predicaments, causes, God, etc., in which diverse material objects, participating snore or less in the formal ratio of being, are explained. As a potential whole, Metaphysics has various functions or offices, e.g., to explain its own proper principles to argue with those who deny its principles or those of other sciences, to draw conclusions from its principles, to determine for the lower sciences their proper object and peculiar method to judge the principles and conclusions of the other sciences, and to employ all the lower sciences in its service.

3. THEOLOGY UNDER THE *Ratio* OF A WHOLE

IN the first place, Theology can in no way take on the nature of a universal whole, nor have subjective parts, because it is one science, with absolute, indivisible unity, from the fact that its formal *ratio sub qua* is indivisible and always the same throughout all its parts. However, it can and de facto does have the formality of an integral whole and of a *totum potestativum.*

The proof that Theology is an integral whole is easy, as long as this is correctly understood, in the sense explained above. Theology is concerned with an almost infinite number of material objects constituting one total or adequate object, namely all of revelation. Thus it includes numerous tracts, of the widest variety, wherein the diverse material objects are examined, e. g. tracts on the One God, the Triune God, the Creator, the angels, man, etc. These tracts are not all of the same importance, but of varying perfection among themselves, according as they participate more or less in the formal *ratio* of Theology, which is the *ratio* of the Deity.

The first and-Most prominent tract of Theology—and, moreover, its principal integral part—is that which treats of God as He is in Himself: the tract on God, One and Triune. Following in order after this tract are others in which diverse objects are considered insofar as they bespeak a formal ordination to God. According as these objects more or less approach to God in this ordination, so do the various tracts which treat of them possess more or less importance. "Everything considered in this science," says the Angelic Doctor, "is either God Himself or things which are from God and ordered to God, precisely under this formality, just as the physician considers signs and causes and many similar things inasmuch as they are in some way related to health. Hence the closer anything approaches to the true nature of the Divinity, so much the more properly (*principalius*) is it considered in this science."[4] No one can fail to perceive that the ratio of *totum potestativum*, or potential whole, is verified in general of Sacred

Theology, for our Theology—one single science—comprises in itself the nature of wisdom and that of science, the perfection of both a speculative and a practical discipline. Therefore, although remaining always one, identical science, Sacred Theology must be able to exercise the various function which correspond to these diverse habits, both of which it includes within its own nature.

II. THE POTENTIAL PARTS OF
SACRED THEOLOGY

ACCORDING to what has been said thus far, the potential parts of Theology are the various activities, functions, or offices which it exercises with regard to its object. In each of these parts the complete nature of. Theology must be reserved not, however, all of its force (*tota ejus virtus*). The whole essence of Theology must be retained, since it is entirely one and the same habit which elicits each and every one of the several activities, but not the complete power of Theology, because this complete power is not actuated in each activity. When it is explaining or defending its principles, Theology is not drawing conclusions, and when it reposes in the sweet contemplation of Divine things, it is not directing one in practical affairs, and so forth.

Nevertheless, all of these parts are intimately and necessarily connected with each other, inasmuch as they are rooted in one and the same habit. They have, further, an essential order and subordination among themselves according as they more or less express and explain the force of the habit by which they are elicited.

Therefore, if they have an intimate connection and necessary subordination among themselves, it follows that they can not be exercised with absolute autonomy or independence, but must be exercised like the several functions of an organic whole, for which the harmonious concurrence of many and various powers is required, that life may be nourished, conserved, and fostered. St. Augustine would seem to refer to these various functions of Theology when he writes: "Only that is attributed to this science whereby our most salutary faith is generated, nourished, defended and strengthened."[5]

Notwithstanding the supreme unity which they enjoy, by reason both of the one principle from which they originate and of the one ultimate end to which they are ordered; the potential parts of Theology do admit of a distinction from one another, for by definition they are functions expressing and making explicit in different

13

ways the power of the habit of Theology. This plurality and diversity arises, not so much from the diversity of material objects as from the ver eminent perfection of the habit, which is able to exercise various offices with respect to its various material objects. For example, Theology explains the mystery of the Incarnation, defends it against adversaries, and draws from it conclusions which were virtually contained in it. "Although this science is one," writes Aquinas himself, "yet it has to do with many things [material object], and is capable of many functions [its eminent power], according to which its parts (*modos*) are to be distinguished."[6]

From this it is evident that, in order to determine the number and nature of the parts of any *totum potestativum*, it is necessary first to define the nature of the whole itself. Hence we infer further that the number of the potential parts of Theology, as well as their nature, cannot be determined unless the nature of the science of Theology is itself previously known.

1. THEOLOGY ACCORDING TO
MODERN AUTHORS

In his conception of the nature of Theology, St. Thomas differs considerably from most modern authors. Modern authors generally conceive of Theology as a science which deduces conclusions from truths formally and explicitly revealed. They construct the whole edifice of theological science on this analogy: Faith stands to Theology in the supernatural order in the same relationship as the habit of first principles stands to the habit of science in the natural order. Theology, then, is related to Faith as science is related to understanding or to the habit of first principles. But science is distinct from understanding: first, because understanding regards truths known *per se* and *immediately*, while science is concerned with truths which are deduced from principles, and so are only mediately evident; secondly, because in the habit of understanding there is simple or adherent; (*adhaesivus*) assent to principles, whereas in

15

science there is discursive assent to conclusions. The first difference arises from the part of the object; the second, from the part of the subject, and is inferred immediately from the first.

The objective reason for assenting to the conclusions is the principles, insofar as these contain the conclusions virtually, or—which is the same thing—the reason is the passive, virtual existence (*continentia passiva et virtualis*) of the conclusions in the principles.

It is quite obvious from all this that science may best be defined by the classic phrase: "the habit of conclusions acquired by demonstration from principles." Theology is to be conceived in this way. Sacred Theology is intimately connected with faith; for it is the science of faith, and yet is distinct from it: first, because faith has to do with truths formally and immediately revealed, whereas Theology is concerned with conclusions drawn from those truths or with truths virtually revealed; secondly, because in faith there is simple assent, "adhesive" or "inhesive" assent, without any discourse, which is

16

elicited by us in virtue of divine revelation, while in Theology assent is based on discourse, which human reason ordains and which proceeds from formally revealed truths to those only virtually revealed. Conformably to the aforesaid analogy, Theology may be defined and, as a matter of fact, is commonly enough defined by the authors, thus: " the habit of conclusions deduced by demonstration from truths formally and immediately revealed."[7] Thus the entire field of divine revelation is adequately divided into two parts. The first part is the field of truths revealed in an explicit and formal manner; faith alone looks to truths of this sort. The other part is the field of truths only virtually revealed, with these only Theology is occupied. Since the science of Theology treats of truths deduced by discourse from revealed doctrine, it is evident that its formal light is virtual revelation or the virtual existence of conclusions in revealed truths, or else the very truths of faith, as they offer these conclusions.[8]

What is commonly maintained by the authors concerning the nature of Theology is all true in itself, and would not be in the least reprehensible, if it were applied to Theology as it is formally a science or under the formal ratio of science. But the error lies precisely in this, that it is predicated of the whole of Theology, whereas it is proper to only a part. An inadmissible transfer is made from the part to the whole, from the qualified to the absolute or unqualified. What is the definition of only a part is put forward as the definition of the whole, with the result that the definition does not equal the thing defined, and for this reason is not a good definition.

From the fact that the whole of Theology deduces conclusions, Gotti and Billuart infer—a legitimate inference—that Positive Theology is either not true Theology, distinct from faith, or else that it too should draw conclusions from revealed truths, and not merely expose and present what has actually been revealed.[9]

From this concept of Theology, various and serious inconveniences follow, both as regards the interpretation of St. Thomas, as well as regards the construction of theological science.

With regard to interpretating the mind of St. Thomas, there are undoubtedly grave difficulties. The Angelic Doctor uses the terms "Theology," "Sacred Doctrine," and "Sacred Scripture," without any distinction, to signify one, identical sacred science,"[10] which would not be legitimate, unless for him Sacred Scripture—and, indeed, whatever has been explicitly and immediately revealed—were also the object of Theology.

Moreover, in the first and introductory question of the entire *Summa Theologiae*, St. Thomas treats of the existence, nature, and method of Sacred Theology as a habit distinct from faith. If Sacred Theology, as distinct from faith, were only concerned with truths virtually revealed, by what right does the Angelic Doctor demonstrate the existence of Theology by proving the necessity of divine revelation, and by what further right, in the last two articles of this question—as it were, abruptly interrupting the context of the whole question—does he

19

ask: " Whether Holy Scripture should use metaphors," and "Whether in Holy Scripture a word may have several senses?"[11] What significance have these articles for a question concerned with the existence, nature, and method of Theology as distinct from faith and from Sacred Scripture?

The incongruities which attend the modern concept are of no less importance for the construction itself of theological science. If the light *sub quo* of Sacred Theology is virtual revelation, it necessarily follows that no question will be properly and formally theological unless it may be considered under this light of virtual revelation, because whatever is not illuminated by the theological light, whatever is not animated and vivified with the theological spirit, is completely foreign to the science of Theology, and the theologian as such cannot occupy himself with it. If he should do so, he will no longer be functioning as a theologian. But what must then be said of the innumerable philosophical problems or truths known solely by the natural light of reason, which are so often encountered in Theology? In the aforesaid concept of Theology, these philosophical propositions are not the proper field of the theologian, except when they are included among the articles of faith in order to draw a certain conclusion, that is: when, in a theological demonstration, one premise is revealed while the other is known only by the natural light of reason. Further, according to this position, whenever in a theological demonstration there is not at least one revealed premise, such a demonstration neither is nor may be truly and properly called theological.

What, then, are we to say about a demonstration of the rational credibility of the mysteries of faith, wherein both premises are naturally known? What about an argument in which the theologian, from truths known absolutely, solves difficulties proposed by adversaries against Divinely revealed truths? Further, what must be said of a question in which the theologian—reflecting on his own proper science—explains and demonstrates its necessity, its nature, and its proper method? What, finally, must we say of the great number of arguments composed of two premises, both of which are known solely by reason, which are employed in Theology? Must we maintain that all these arguments do not pertain to the theologian, and that, if he should ever concern himself with them, the theologian is straying outside the limits of his .province?

Vasquez answers this last question in the affirmative,[12] contrary to the more common opinion of theologians. His position—although false—nevertheless appears as conformable to and following logically from the doctrine which would assign virtual revelation as the light *sub quo* of Theology. A conclusion deduced by a demonstration in which no premise is revealed is, to be sure, not inferred from revealed truths: therefore, it was not contained in them. Hence the reason for assenting to this sort of conclusion cannot be virtual revelation nor, consequently, did the demonstration proceed under the light of virtual revelation.

2. THEOLOGY ACCORDING TO ST. THOMAS

The true nature of Theology, according to the mind of St. Thomas, is expressed in the following analogy: As understanding stands to wisdom, so does faith in relation to Theology.[13] Therefore, Theology will bear the same relation towards faith which wisdom does to the habit of first principles. The analogy then: wisdom is compared to understanding as a *fuller* and *more universal knowledge*,[14] for, in the first place, wisdom regards the first principles themselves in order to explain and defend them, wherein it agrees with the habit of first principles; and moreover, it draws conclusions from principles, wherein it departs from the role of understanding and takes on the ratio of science. Wisdom then has two distinct functions: first, that of explaining and defending principles; and secondly, that of inferring conclusions. In the exercise of the first function, wisdom attains the object which is proper to understanding, namely, principles or truths which are *per se* and immediately evident. In the exercise of its other function, wisdom attains the object which is proper to science, namely, truths which are known mediately or by demonstration. Therefore, the object of wisdom is broader (*amplius*) than the objects both of understanding and of science taken separately. It is broader than the object of understanding because it extends to conclusions, which the habit of first principles does not touch; it is equally wider than the object of science, because it embraces principles, which science does not attain.

Although principles are attained both by understanding and by wisdom, they are not grasped by each in the same way. Understanding grasps principles by simple assent, without any discourse; wisdom, however, is concerned with the same principles, but in a discursive and argumentative mode.

Now, then, if Theology be conceived as wisdom in relation to faith, by this very fact it must be admitted that the theological habit should not only draw conclusions from the truths of faith, but also should explain and defend these very truths. From this it follows that the *total* or *adequate* material object of Theology is not truth which is only *virtually* revealed, but *every revealed truth whatsoever*, whether formally and explicitly or mediately and virtually revealed. In a word, it embraces both principles and conclusions. Therefore, the object of Theology is *broader* in scope than is the object of faith. Further, faith and Theology are not to be distinguished because the former regards truths formally and immediately revealed, whereas the latter treats only of those which have been virtually revealed. The true distinction between faith and Theology lies in this, that faith is concerned only with what has been immediately and explicitly revealed, and Theology is concerned with truths which have been revealed both immediately and formally as well as mediately and virtually.

It must be noted that faith and Theology do not both treat in the same manner of truths immediately revealed. Faith seizes these revealed truths by a simple assent based solely on the authority of God revealing, without any discourse, but Theology grasps these truths by means of human discourse. The formal, motivating object in the habit of faith is formal revelation; in Theology it is human discourse, under the light of divine revelation. According to this conception, Theology is at once an explication, a defense, and an unfolding of faith itself, objectively considered.

What precisely is the light *sub quo* of Theology thus conceived? The best answer to this question is that, as regards the drawing of conclusions—that is, taking Theology under the formal ratio of a science—its light is virtual revelation, because, in deducing conclusions, a revealed truth virtually containing other truths is assumed as a principle of discourse. This revealed truth, as it implies a conclusion, is virtual revelation. This is plainly evident and is very clearly deduced from the concept itself of a science which discourses or draws conclusions from revealed truths.

Further, what is the light of Theology when the latter is exercising its sapiential function of explaining and defending its own principles. Without a doubt, it can at times explain and defend these principles under the light of virtual revelation, as it does when, from one truth explicitly revealed concerning a mystery, it argues the proof of another mystery, also elsewhere explicitly revealed.

However, it is no less certain that when the theologian explains divine mysteries by analogy with things of nature, adducing various arguments of convenience, as is so often done in Theology, and when he demonstrates that such a truth is explicitly taught in Sacred Scripture or has been solemnly defined by a certain Council; indeed, when he proves the rational credibility of the mysteries of faith, when he expounds the intimate nature of the very science of Theology, when he passes judgment on truth arrived at by the human sciences—in these and in similar functions, the theologian is not inferring any conclusion from revelation. Consequently, he is not proceeding under the light of virtual revelation. What then shall we say? When the theologian performs all of these functions, is he not touching on true

Theology? He most certainly is; when he fulfills all of these offices, he is both a true theologian and is treating of matters which are truly theological. Will Theology then have one light insofar as it is a science and another insofar as it assumes the ratio of wisdom? Such contrived devising is far from our concept of reality! Theology can have but one, identical light, whether it exercise the function of wisdom or carry out that of science.

Sacred Theology is a habit which stands mid-way between faith and natural Theology, which is a part of philosophy. Therefore, it will have a light which is a mean between the light of faith and that of natural Theology. Now the light of faith is the supernatural light of divine revelation; while the light of natural Theology is that of pure reason. Therefore the intermediate light is one which partakes both of revelation and of reason: it is *the natural light of reason exercised under the light of divine revelation.*

Modern authors generally carry this doctrine further, and subsume: But the natural light of reason, exercised under the light of Divine Revelation, is the same as virtual revelation. Therefore virtual revelation is the light *sub quo* of Sacred Theology. Now in this last inference there lies concealed—unless we are seriously mistaken—an enormous equivocation. It is absolutely true and certain that, in virtual revelation, the two lights mentioned above are connected with each other--with, however, a certain subordination of one to the other—in the function of deducing conclusions. The fact is, in all truth, that the union of these two lights, concurring simultaneously and with due subordination in arriving at the knowledge of some truth, is effected not only in virtual revelation, but also in a thousand and one other instances, e. g., in all demonstrations wherein; although both premises be known solely from natural reason both premises and the entire demonstration proceed under the *positive direction of faith*. In these instances nothing is concluded *from faith*, but the conclusions *are* drawn *under the light of faith;* nothing is inferred *from revelation*, but inference is made *under the light of revelation.*

29

Hence the concursus of natural reason with and under the light of divine revelation is evidently broader in its scope than virtual revelation. Therefore, when one concludes that the union of natural reason and the light of revelation must equal virtual revelation, an illicit jump has been made from the whole to the part, from the unqualified (*simpliciter*) to the qualified (*secundum quid*). This very leap is made by the authors, because of the overly-restricted—and hence imperfect—concept which they have of Theology which is accepted by them only under the formal ratio of science. From this point of view, it is indeed true that the two lights considered as occurring in the educing of a conclusion from revealed truths cannot so concur, sinless they be arranged as two distinct premises of a theological demonstration. But this is to narrow the concept of Theology snore than may justly be allowed. The light sub quo of Theology in its total extension is the natural light of reason, exercised under the light of divine revelation, or under the positive direction of faith; it is "reason guided by faith,"—as our Angelic Doctor writes[15]—or "reason illumined by faith," in the classic expression used by the Vatican Council.[16] This subordinate concursus of natural reason with the light of divine revelation pervades the whole, of Theology and directs all its functions, although, it differs slightly—by mere accidental diversity, to be sure—in the exercise of various functions, conformably to the peculiar nature of each function to be exercised. As often as it is a question of drawing a certain conclusion from revealed truths, these two lights must concur by way of virtual revelation, not precisely in order to preserve the nature of true Theology, but rather in order to safeguard its character as an *inference from revealed truths*. When however, it is not a question of this type of deduction, the two lights need not be ordered in the aforesaid manner.

One might possibly confront us with the objection that, when Theology exercises its sapiential function, it is properly and formally *discursive*, for otherwise it would be indistinguishable from faith, which is simple assent to truths divinely revealed. But every discourse proceeds from one truth to another. Therefore, Sacred Theology—even in the exercise of its office as wisdom—should always discourse from one revealed truth to another.

Contrary to the opinion of a few theologians—Molina being one of them[17]—we grant that, in the case cited, Theology is also properly and formally *discursive*, and not merely *adhesive*.

But it is one thing to discourse *from* articles of faith, and a tremendously different thing to discourse *about* articles of faith, under the *light of divine revelation*. In order to be distinguished from faith, the habit of Theology must be truly *discursive*; but it does not necessarily follow from this that it must discourse *from* the articles of faith, but either *from* or *about* these articles. Discoursing about articles of faith suffices to preserve the distinction of Theology from faith, when both habits treat of the same material object.

The inconveniences which logical reasoning saw involved in the opposite and more common concept of Theology are best explained from the concept of Theology just delineated. First, let us consider the consequences which opposed the correct interpretation of the mind of St. Thomas. If the total and adequate object of Theology is everything which has been revealed, both formally and immediately (as what is contained in Sacred Scripture) , as well as virtually (as what is deduced by legitimate demonstration from truths explicitly revealed)', it is not a cause for astonishment that the same habit of Theology may sometimes be denominated by its total object and called "sacred doctrine;" or again by its partial, although more proper (*principaliori*) object, in which case it is called "Sacred Scripture;" or, lastly, by its partial and less proper object, in which case it is designated as the "Science of Theology."

Furthermore: The plain and obvious way to demonstrate the necessity and the existence of Theology is to prove the existence of some object which can and must be explained by human discursive reasoning, but which de facto neither is nor can be attained by any humanly devised sciences. The logical conclusion will be that there does exist divine and supernatural revelation, which can and should be interpreted, explained, defended, and unfolded by human (intellectual, speculative) ingenuity. The science which interprets, explains, defends and unfolds divine revelation is Sacred Theology. Therefore, Sacred Theology exists and is necessary.

The nature of this science cannot be determined merely by the relation it bears to its partial object (as, sc., conclusions) by demonstrating that it has the ratio of science, that it is one, practical, the noblest of all sciences, demonstrative (*argumentative*) , etc. Theology's ordination to the other part of its object must also be adverted to, and this is to truths immediately and formally revealed, which are contained in Sacred Scripture, and which, moreover, Sacred Theology undertakes to interpret, explain, and defend. Hence we should not be surprised that St. Thomas, in determining the nature of Theology, pauses for a short space in order to explain the proper language and peculiar senses of Sacred Scripture. In fact it would have been more surprising if—having conceived Theology as wisdom in a true and formal sense—he had failed to say a word about the sources (*principiis*), the interpretation, explanation, and defense of which Theology ought to undertake. The principles of Theology are contained especially in Sacred Scripture. Thus there is no rupture in the context of the first and introductory question of the entire *Summa Theologiae*, when the Angelic Doctor proceeds (immediately) from the first to the second article, nor when, from the eighth, he passes on to the ninth and tenth. That everything which is touched upon in this question has to be treated, follows from the intimate nature of Theology as it is a true and formal wisdom.[18]

This concept of Theology fits in perfectly with what the historians tell us of the manner in which Theology was expounded by the Masters at the University of Paris in the thirteenth century, among them, St. Thomas himself; namely by way of a commentary on Sacred Scriptures.[19]

But, let us turn now to consider those other inconveniences which were cited against the very structure of theological science. For the various functions enumerated above to be truly theological, nothing is required other than that they be exercised under the light of divine revelation or under the positive direction of faith. In the order of nature living bodies are nourished by taking in from the outside elements which are extrinsic to themselves. Once these elements have been incorporated and assimilated to the living organism, they are vivified and informed by the same soul and with the same life which the living supposit itself enjoys. In a similar manner, Theology—on account of the deficiency of the subject in which it is exercised—receives from philosophy many elements which are, absolutely speaking, extraneous to itself, but which it incorporates and assimilates to itself by informing, animating, and vivifying them with its own proper life and its own peculiar spirit.

Wherefore, these elements, when examined materially, are philosophical and extraneous; but, considered formally, they are truly and properly theological. They are proper to Theology as its ministers (*sunt propria Theologiae ministerialiter*), to borrow Cajetan's phrase,[20] because they are changed from foreign to proper in order to minister to Theology and to supply for the defect of the theologian. The soul and spirit of Theology, with which these elements must be informed, is its formal *quod* and *quo* object. For this reason, the elements which are derived from philosophy should be considered in their relations to those things which are theological by their very nature; or, in other words, in their ordination to God (the formal *quod* object). Moreover, they ought to be studied or grasped under the light of divine revelation, under the positive direction of faith (formal object *sub quo*). All that we have maintained, therefore, appears to be perfectly harmonious both with the objective truth of things and with the mind of St. Thomas in his treatment of these matters.

The adequate definition of Theology, according to both objective truth and to the mind of St. Thomas, can be formulated thus: "Discursive wisdom, exercised under the light of divine revelation, on every truth revealed by God either immediately and formally or mediately and virtually." Theology is called, in the first place, "wisdom," which in itself embraces simultaneously the ratio both of science and of understanding, since it both deduces conclusions and concerns itself with the very principles. We say "discursive," that Theology may be clearly distinguished from both faith and the gift of wisdom. "Under the light of divine revelation" distinguishes Theology from purely human wisdom, which is called Metaphysics. "Concerning every truth divinely revealed" indicates the two-fold material object of Theology. Briefly, it may be said that Theology is the *Metaphysics of Revelation* or the *Metaphysics of faith.*

To the above we may add that this wisdom—unlike purely natural wisdom—is at the same time speculative and practical, and more speculative than practical. This may be deduced immediately and by most formal inference from the fact that, of the principles which it examines and out of which it draws conclusions, some are speculative while others are practical. Now a science will assume the same capacity as the principle from which it proceeds. This two-fold character of Theology can be proved also from the fact that our Theology is a certain participation in the divine science,[21] which is at once speculative and practical, and primarily speculative rather than practical.[22] It is proved lastly—and this is the basic and formal reason—from the fact that the formal object of Theology, which is God, is at the same time the supreme truth which is to be contemplated and the supreme good which is to be desired and loved.[23]

3. THE POTENTIAL PARTS OF THEOLOGY

ONCE the nature of Theology has been determined, there is little or no difficulty in discovering the number and function of its potential parts. In discerning these parts we must distinguish carefully between that whence the faculty of supplying some necessity arises and that from which the necessity or need of seeking or receiving aid itself originates. Always, in all instances, the faculty and the need will mutually correspond, as active and passive principles. The faculty of supplying a necessity arises always from the perfection and intensity of the habit, for a thing acts only insofar as it is perfect, insofar as it is in act. Need or indigence, on the .contrary, is born of the poverty or imperfection of a subject, for a thing is passive (*patitur*) insofar as it is in potency.

Theology uses the lower sciences, explains and defends its own principles, on account of the infirmity of our intellect or in order to come to the aid of our intellectual dullness.[24] However, it can supply this need of ours from its own abundance or powerful resources. Hence the faculty or power of exercising these functions flows from the force of the theological habit; whereas the need of receiving these services or functions results from the weakness of our intellect, in which the habit of Theology resides as in a subject. With this much granted, let us see now how both the number and the function of the potential parts of Sacred Theology can be demonstrated.

Our Theology can be considered (1) in relation to its object, (2) in relation to its subject, (3) in its own internal ordination (*in ordine ad se ipsam*), or (4) in relation to the other sciences. Indeed, every science is a habit which perfects the intellect and orders it to a knowledge of some determined object. Therefore it is an entity which is distinct from both subject and object, although it regards both of these. For this reason, every habit can be considered either in its absolute entity, or with respect to its relationship with either its subject or its object. Furthermore, it can also be considered in comparison with the other habits, of which it stands in some need. From this we conclude that the various functions which are proper to Theology will necessarily pertain to it in the form of one of the four relationships enumerated above. Certain functions, then, will belong to Theology with respect to its object; others with respect to its subject; still others with respect to the science itself; and others, finally, in comparison with the other, human sciences.

1. *The Functions of Theology With Respect to its Own Proper Object.*

Theology—as a wisdom—has a two-fold material object: (1) the truths formally revealed, i. e. the articles of faith, which sacred doctrine ought to explain and defend; (2) the truths virtually revealed in their principles, which the theologian should draw out. Hence we have determined already the two general functions of Theology with respect to its object; (1) to explain and defend its own proper principles and, (2) to deduce conclusions from these principles. Of these two functions, the first is sapiential, while the second is properly scientific. The sapiential office has not only to explain or only to defend: it must explain and at the same time defend, because—since contraries share the same ratio—" it belongs to the same subject both to pursue one of two contraries and to refute the other; as medicine brings about health while it dispels illness.[25]

The principles of Theology are those truths which we believe by the habit of supernatural and Divine faith. But in every act of faith we always believe three things: (1) we believe that God has revealed something or has spoken to men (divine revelation is that by which we believe divine mysteries and is at the same time that which we believe) ; (2) we believe the *nexus* between divine revelation and the object manifested by it, e. g. we believe that God has revealed that the Divine Word was made flesh, was crucified, died and was buried, etc.; (3) we believe the truth revealed by God or the mystery divinely made known to us, e. g. that God is one and three, that the Divine Word is incarnate, etc.

Three things, then, are believed by us in every act of faith: (1) an objective or ontological supernatural truth, a certain Divine mystery; (2) this truth has been revealed. by God, for we assent to it in virtue of this divine revels tion; (3) the fact or existence of Divine Revelation manifesting the aforesaid truth. We believe that God is one and triune (the objective divine truth), because God has so revealed (the fact of revelation and the nexus between revelation and the Trinity of Persons in the numerically one Divine Essence.)

Therefore, Sacred Theology—in its sapiential function—should undertake to explain and defend those three things, which are believed as principles in every act of faith: (1) the fact of divine revelation, (2) the connection between God's revelation and the truth which is believed to have been revealed, and (3) the revealed truth itself. The fact of divine Revelation is explained by exposing the nature of divine revelation, its possibility, and its convenience. It is defended, (1) positively, by proving its reasonable credibility by means of the various motives of credibility and, (2) negatively, by refuting all the arguments proposed either against its possibility, nature, or convenience, or against the fact or existence of divine revelation. This is all accomplished in Apologetics, which is one of the potential parts of Sacred Theology.

Theology ought, moreover, to explain and to defend the connection between divine revelation and the truths divinely revealed. In other words, it ought to explain and defend what has been actually revealed and the sense in which it has been revealed. But this will be impossible unless the sources or fonts wherein divine revelation is certainly and faithfully contained, are first known, together with the other sources hi which a certain and legitimate interpretation of divine revelation is to be found. Hence Theology, in exercising this function, should first ascertain and defend the fonts of divine revelation, and this it does in the "Methodology of Positive Theology" which, therefore, is also a true potential part of Theology. After this, Theology should explain and defend what is held as certainly revealed by God in each of the sources mentioned above. In this consists the proper office of Positive Theology which, according to the diversity of the sources it examines, is termed biblical, symbolic, patristic, etc.

It is also a sapiential function of Theology to explain and defend divinely revealed mysteries, that is, their innermost, objective truth or nature, so that we may obtain some understanding of them. In the carrying out of this task, Theology must treat first its own peculiar method of defending divine mysteries in general, that is, the manner in which they can be explained by analogy with natural things and through their connection with each other and with man's ultimate end,[26] as well as how objections raised against these mysteries may be answered either from truths of faith or even from things naturally known, either in a certain regard or absolutely.[27] Lastly, Theology should explain and defend each of the mysteries of faith according to the rules which have been previously established in its prior functions. This office is the sapiential function of Scholastic Theology.

In the joint application and defense of all the aforesaid, the sapiential function of Theology with respect to its own proper object is carried out. The function of Theology as a science is to deduce conclusions from revealed principles. In carrying out this office it must treat first of the structure and laws of theological deduction, and then proceed to draw from the several principles (of faith) the conclusions virtually contained in them.

2. The Functions of Theology With Respect to its Subject.

Every science is a certain perfection of the intellect; some are perfections of the speculative intellect, while others are perfections of the practical intellect, according to the attainment or exigency of the nature of their object. When the object of a science is of such a nature and in such a condition that it can in no way be brought into effect or touched to some extent by our action, then the science which is concerned with the knowledge of this sort of object must be said to be absolutely speculative. When the object of a science is something which can be done or made (*factible*) or is to some extent attainable by our operation, then the science concerned with that object is both said to be and is practical. Therefore, a science is said to be either speculative or practical from the nature of the object as it stands with regard to 'the subject. Thus, a science concerned with one and the same object is practical or speculative according to the subject with which the object is compared. The science of natural things is speculative with regard to man and practical with regard to God.

From what has been said above, it is seen that Theology is both speculative and practical. Therefore, with respect to the intellect—which it perfects—it will exercise two different functions: it will direct reason in the contemplation of divine truth and in regulating all of our activity in order to attain the end which is eternal life.[28] These are the two functions which are exercised in Dogmatic and in Moral Theology, respectively.

Moral Theology can consider the morality of human acts, either in the universal (General Moral) or in particular (Special Moral). It can consider them in particular, either indistinctly, under the formality of moral good and evil (casuistics), or under the single formality of moral good. In the latter case, it considers human acts either as goods to be effected through supernatural means which are proportionate to man himself, namely, the virtues (Ascetical) , or through supernatural principles which operate in a divine mode, namely, the gifts (Mystical) .[29]

3. *The Functions of Theology With Respect to Itself as a Science.*

In the natural order or in the field of philosophy, it does not pertain to the particular sciences themselves to determine the nature, division, properties, and peculiar method of the sciences, but this is the function of the supreme science among them, which, since it is the head and queen of all, from the fact that it is wisdom, both can and should assign to each of them its own proper object and define the boundaries beyond which the considerations of each may not extend.[30] Theology, however, since it is the supreme science and true wisdom, should reflect upon itself and explain its own proper nature, its properties, and its peculiar method, utilizing to this end all those doctrines which are ordinarily treated in Logic concerning the nature and division of demonstration, of science, of method, etc. This is the only function which Theology exercises in its own regard.

4. The Functions of Theology With Respect to the Other, Human Sciences.

With respect to the human sciences, St. Thomas attributes to Theology three different functions: (1) to judge all human sciences, both as regards their principles and as regards their conclusions, (2) to order or direct all the philosophical sciences and, (3) to use all of them.[31]

These three functions are proper to wisdom in relation to inferior sciences.[32] Now Theology is truly and properly a wisdom, and more so even than Metaphysics.[33] Therefore, the three functions mentioned above must be attributed to sacred Theology with respect to all the philosophical sciences, even to Metaphysics itself.

It is indeed 'true that "lesser things are to be guided by higher causes,"[34] and that the final and supreme judgment of things is through the ultimate and supreme sense. Sacred Theology considers God as He is the first existing Truth (*prima veritas in essendo*), the cause and norm of all created truth. Hence it belongs to Theology to judge all created truth. "Whatever is found in other sciences contrary to a truth of this science must be condemned as entirely false."[35]

Moreover, when there are several arts or sciences ordered in such a way that the end of some of them is subordinated to the end of others, then that science or art which treats of the end to which the ends of the other sciences or arts are ordained, is architectonic with respect to all the others, and, to it pertains the office of ordering or directing all the lower sciences and of using them in its service. And "thus, since the end of the art of pharmacy, which is the concoction of remedies, is ordained to the end of the art of medicine, which is health, the physician directs the pharmacist, and uses for his own purposes the remedies mixed by the latter."[36] But the end of the whole of philosophy falls under the end of Theology and is ordained to it. Therefore, it is the office of Theology to order or command the whole of philosophy and to use it in its service."[37]

The relation of philosophy to Theology is like that of the civil state to the Church. The civil society has its own proper end, which, however, is ordered to the superior end of the Church. In a similar manner, philosophy has its own proper end within its own sphere, but this end is ordered to the higher end of Theology.

Theology can use all human sciences as inferiors and servants in the exercise of its function. Some of these sciences may be more useful than others, according to exigencies of the special function to be undertaken. When these human sciences are employed in the service of Theology, they are informed and animated with the spirit of Theology, inasmuch as they are ordered to the consideration of theological truths and proceed under the light of divine revelation; they are proper to Theology in the capacity of minsters.[38]

CONCLUSION

I T does not seem possible to admit any other function besides those outlined above. All of these functions are true potential parts of Theology; therefore, in all of them the complete essence of Theology is preserved, for in their exercise human reason always discourses about or from. revealed truths, under the light of divine revelation. However, the complete power of Theology is not retained in each of these functions; is found more or less in some than in others. These same functions are distinct from one another, although they are certainly not independent of one another, but most intimately conjoined and connected.

Consequently, only he can be called a perfect theologian who possesses the habit of Theology not only in its essence but also in all of its powers. For this reason, he and he alone is to be called a perfect theologian who is able to exercise all the functions of Theology, readily, skillfully, and with ease. Thus did Francis de Vitoria conceive of the perfect theologian: "The office and function of the theologian is so extensive that no argument, no dispute, no place seems foreign to the theological profession and institution. And perhaps this is also the reason, as Cicero says of the orator, that in every field of learning and in all the arts there are so few outstanding and eminent men to be found; for such—unless my standards are too stringent—is the great scarcity of good, solid theologians. But Theology is first among all the world's disciplines and studies. Wherefore, it would not seem strange, if not many experts are to be found in a science so very difficult."[39]

Vitoria's disciple, Melchior Cano, has something not unlike his master's to say: "In my opinion, no one could be an accomplished theologian, deserving of the highest praise, unless he had mastered the sciences which treat of all these (theological) courses, and were prepared to use them in ready and skillful argument."[40]

Kindred sentiments are found in the writings of Natalis Alexander: "I will allow that a man is scarcely half a theologian who, although well-versed in scholastic questions, is a stranger, or has only a passing acquaintance, in the fields of sacred Scripture, ecclesiastical History, the Councils, and the teachings of the holy Fathers."[41]

Who is the theologian who can exercise each and every one of the functions of Theology as readily, so skillfully, and so easily? *"Far and from the uttermost coasts is the price of him!"* The great theologians themselves, almost overwhelmed by the magnitude of their science, have openly confessed their ignorance. That great restorer of Theology in Spain, Francis de Vitoria, after forty years spent in preparing lectures afterwards to be delivered in the schools, sensing that his life was drawing to a close, spoke these words to his disciples, almost groaning as he spoke: "It used to seem to me, at the beginning of my career (as a teacher) , after I had completed my course as a student of Theology, that I knew a great deal; but now, to tell the truth, I see that I am still at the threshold. My age and the arduousness of the task terrify me, for I realize that in twenty or thirty years a theologian can know very little, since, in order to be, I will not say a perfect theologian, but one who has some correct understanding of theological matters, a man must study the entire Bible and the commentaries of the Saints on it, which certainly cannot be accomplished in less than a great number of years."[42] Cano expressed himself similarly: "But you may ask: Is there anyone so inflated with error as to persuade himself that he knows (all) these things? In fact, I would not in the least condemn a theologian who had not mastered all of this learning; but I would reprehend one who, although he had not attained the mastery, usurped for himself the title of theologian. For that type of argument, which is aptly drawn from all possible sources, is perfect and complete and includes all factors, nor can it be devised by any save the finished theologian."[43] Dominic Banez shared these same sentiments when he wrote: "Therefore, let no one—no matter with how lofty a genius he may have been endowed and allowed to partake of divine doctrine—think that he is no longer to be counted in the ranks of little children. In truth, is he is truly wise, so much the more will he acknowledge that he is but a little babe. For when a man has finished, then he will begin. Indeed, I find this difference between the most outstanding theologians and the common men among the faithful, that the wiser a theologian is, so much the more earnestly does he acknowledge his own ignorance and infirmity, so that in his own eyes he appears to be a small child. On the other hand, those who have a lesser knowledge of divine science, do not know how much they actually lack, so that they are ignorant of their own ignorance."[44]

I am aware that the goal to be attained by the theologian is surpassingly exalted and sublime. Still, it is the one and only goal towards which we must all strive, unceasingly and with all our strength. But the higher and more sublime the goal, so much the greater, more perservering, and more intense ought our labor to be, so that we might at least draw near to it. Only those courageous souls can approach this goal who have, as it were, carved on their minds and hearts these words of our Angelic Doctor: "Since man's perfection consists in union with God, man should, by all the means in his power, mount up and strive to attain divine truths, so that his intellect may take delight in contemplation, and his reason in the investigation of the things of God, according to the prayer in Ps. 72: 27: It is good for us to adhere to my God '."[45]

Finis

Endnotes

1.

"It must be observed that there are three types of whole. One is universal, which is present to each part in its complete essence and power; hence it is properly predicated of its parts, as when we say: man is an animal. A second type is an integral whole, which is found in any one of its parts neither in its full essence nor by virtue of its total power; in no way, then, it is predicated of a part, for example: a wall is not a house. A third type of whole is a potential whole, which is a mean between the other two; for it is present to each of its parts in its complete essence, but not in all its power. Consequently, it is predicated in a manner which is midway between that of the other. two types: for it is sometimes predicated of its parts, but not properly." *De Spiritualibus Creaturis*, a. 3, ad 3. Cf. also *I Sent.*, a. 3, q. 4, a. C Ad 1; *II Sent.*, d. 9, q. 1, a. 3. ad 1; *IV Sent.*, d. 16, q. 1, a. 1, sol 3; Quodl. 10, q. 3, a. 5; *Summa Theol.*, I, q. 77, a. 1, ad 1; q. 76, a. 8. On the division of parts, cf. *III Sent.*, d. 33, q. 3, a. 1, sol. 1; *Summa Theol.*, q. 48, a. un; q. 130, a. 2; q. 128, a. un; q. 143, a. on; III, q. 90, a. 2; a. 3, corp. et ad 3; *Q. D. De Anima*, a. 10; *De Spir. Creat.*, a. 4.

2.

"If then we consider a habit as to the extent of its object, we shall find a certain multiplicity therein. But since this multiplicity is directed to one thing, on which the habit is chiefly intent, it follows that a habit is a simple quality, not composed of several habits, even though it may extend to many things. For a habit does not extend to many things save in relation to [*in ordine ad*] one, whence it derives

it derives its unity." *Summa Theol.*, q. 54, a. 4.

3.

Ibid., I-II,q. 57, a. 2 ad 1 and ad 2; q. 66, a. 5, ad 4.

4.

In I Sent., q. I, Prolog., a. 4.

5.

De Trinitate, XIV, ch. 1 (in PL XLII, 1037)

6.

In I Sent., q. I, Prolog., a. 5, ad 5.

7.

"Acquired Theology is that which is obtained by one's own labor and study, through discourse, whereby some truth is reached from principles revealed in and believed on divine faith, such that those who possess it are today commonly called theologians, and which, since it is proper. to wayfarers, will be the chief question which concerns us here. In other words, Theology is the science which reasons from revealed principles, believed on divine faith. This science, as I have said, is divided into Positive and Scholastic; and both of these are divided into Moral, Polemical, and Mystical." Gotti, *Theologia Scholastico-Dogmatica*, Tract. I Isag., q. I, Dub. 1, #1, n. viii.

Thus the "The doctrine of divine things, deducing conclusions from imme diately revealed principles of faith." Billuart, Dissert. Prooemialis de Sacra Doctrine, a. T.

"The discipline, which, from revealed principles, draws a multitude of conclusions about God and about everything which is in some way related to Him." P. Cerboni, O. P., *Institutiones Theologicae*, Disp. I, cap. I, p. 2.

"The science of God and of divine things, acquired from principles divinely revealed." Mazzelle, S. J., *Praelectiones Scholastico-Dogrnaticae*, f, Proleg, h. 5.

"The science of God and of divine things, deducing conclusions discursively from faith and the principles believed on faith." Hugon, O. P., *Tractatus Dogmatica*, I, Qu. prooem. art. I, n. III.

"The science which, with the aid of reason, from the principles of faith, draws certain conclusions about God and things in some

way related to Slim." Valentine of the
Assumption, O.C.D., *Theologia Dogmatico-
Scholastica*, Vol. I, p. 14, n. 2. Zubizarreta's
definition is the same as Valentine's, cf.
Theologia Dogmatica-Scholastics, I, a. I, n. 2.
"Theology is certain knowledge or science
concerning divine things proceeding from
revealed principles." Daffara, O. P., *De Deo
uno et trino*, q. I, p. 2, n. 2.

8.

"Virtual revelation, i. e. the virtual existence
(*continentia*) of conclusions in the principles
of faith which are formally revealed, is the
reason for assenting to the conclusions
drawn from such principles; nor do we have
any other term which might signify in an
incomplex way this formal nature or ratio of
theology . . . when the principles of faith are
considered insofar as they present
conclusions, they constitute the formal
nature of Theology in its character of a light
of knowledge (*luminis scibilis*) and of virtual
revelation. However, they manifest by
inference (*illativo modo*) and not in a simple
manner those truths which are virtually
contained in and can be deduced from the
truths revealed by faith." John of St. Thomas,
Cursus Theologicus, tom. I, p. 377b, 378a-b.

9.

"For if Positive Theology were not

argumentative, it would not be Theology, which is essentially the habit whereby conclusions can be deduced and known from revealed principles. Nor would it differ from faith, since the Theology of wayfarers differs from faith in this, that faith believes, without discourse, things revealed by God, whereas Theology discourses from or concerning revealed doctrines." Gotti, *op. cit.*, q. I, Dub. II, #1, n. V.

"Therefore, Positive and Scholastic Theology do not differ essentially and objectively from each other, for they have the same object, but they differ only accidentally, by reason of their diverse methods. And so they are deceived who confine Positive Theology to a knowledge of the revealed truths contained in Scripture, Tradition, etc. . . .while they reduce Scholastic Theology to the discursive deduction of conclusions from revealed truths. If this were the case, then Positive Theology would be indistinguishable from faiths, it would not be Theology, as is clear from the definition of the latter. Therefore, Positive Theology does indeed discourse and infer and deduce other truths from revealed principles—although not so rigidly (accurate) as Scholastic Theology, and in this alone do they differ." Billuart, *loc. cit.*

10.

"We ask further whether [sacred doctrine] is one science. And it would seem that it is not.

For no science is concerned with particulars. But in sacred Scripture the deeds of particular men, such as Abraham, Isaac, etc., are treated. Therefore, . . . On the contrary: According to Augustine, Theology is the science of the things which pertain to man's salvation." *1 Sent.*, q. I, Prolog. art. S.

"Whether in the science of faith, which concerns God, it is lawful to use the rational arguments of philosophers . . .Thus, in *sacred doctrine* we may make a three-fold use of philosophy. . . Nevertheless, those who use philosophy in *Sacred Scripture* can err in two ways. . . . Hence, those who use philosophic arguments in *Sacred Scripture*, by subjecting them . . insofar as sacred doctrine uses physical arguments for their own sakes." *In Boet. De Trinitate*, q. e, art, 5, corp. and ad 5, ad 8.

"But of another sort is that science which considers divine things for their own sakes, as its subject, and this is the Theology which is called Sacred Scripture. . . The Theology which is Sacred Scripture treats of separated beings in the first manner. . . The divine science which is received by divine inspiration has not the Angels for its subject, but (treats of them) only inasmuch as they are taken to manifest that subject. Hence Sacred Scripture treats of Angels as it does of all other creatures." *Ibid.*, q. 5, art. 4, corp. and ad 3.

"Whether Sacred doctrine is a science. . . . No

65

science deals with individual facts, such as the deeds of Abraham, Isaac, and Jacob, and such like. Therefore, sacred doctrine is not a science. . . In reply to the second objection, individual facts are treated of in sacred doctrine, not because it is principally concerned with them; but they are introduced . . . in order to establish the authority of those men through whom the divine revelation, on which this sacred scripture or doctrine is based, has come down to us." Summa Theol., I, q. 1, a. 2, obj. 2 and ad 2.

" Further, *sacred doctrine* is a practical science." *Ibid.*, art. 4 ,obj. 2. "'Whether God is the subject of this science. Whatever conclusions are reached in any science must be comprised under the subject of the science. But in *Sacred Scripture* we reach conclusions not only concerning God, but concerning many other things, such as creatures and human morals. Therefore, God is not the subject of this science, . . In reply to the second objection, whatever conclusions are reached in *sacred doctrine* are considered in their reference to God, not as part or species or accidents (of God) , but as in some way related to Him." *Ibid.*, art. 7, obj. 2 and ad 2.

11.

Concerning this ambiguity, otherwise rather inoffensive, and this limited conception of sacred doctrine, a second case is more notable; it is the very fact that in a question treating of the nature of theological ' science,' there are two long articles on the literary genre of Scripture (whether Sacred Scripture should use metaphors, a. 9) , and on its rules of interpretation (whether Sacred Scripture may have many senses for a single word, a. 10) . It is clear that there we find matter concerning the very establishment of revealed data and the articles of faith, which are the principles of theological science; it is, therefore, matter which is presupposed to the ' science,' the method of which one here wishes to discern, and not to establish the data. Moreover, especially after articles e and 8, the modern reader notices the break in context as he approaches article 9, which has to do with the aptness of the metaphorical style of the Bible." P. Chenu, O. P., " La Theologie conune science au XIII siecle," in *Archives d'histoire doctrinale et litteraire du moyen age,* 1927, pp. 68, 69.

12.

"Nor are the principles of philosophy proper to the theologian except when they are employed in articles of faith to infer some conclusion." *Commentaria ac disputationes in Prim am Partem S. Thomae*, q. 1, a. 8, Disp. XL cap. III, n. 6. " In order to defend Theology as one science, it must be said that it does not pertain to it to treat of moral matters which imply conclusions solely from natural

principles; for this type of demonstration has
its own principles, diverse from those of
Theology, and deduces evident conclusions.
Hence our Theology, that it may retain its
unity as a science, must always argue from
one revealed and one naturally known
principle. On this account, therefore, I
consider Theology as subalternated to moral
philosophy, not absolutely, i. e., not in every
demonstration, but partially, because it
assumes, for some of its conclusions,
premises which are proved in moral
philosophy." *Ibid.*, art. 3, Disp. VII, cap. 5, n.
10. "If those who deny articles of faith admit
none of these (theological) principles, there is
no argument against them within the scope
of Theology, but the latter must serve only to
refute their objections, as St. Thomas
observes expressly in the third conclusion.
For this reason, the later Thomists held that
those arguments by which the credibility of
our faith, is proved, do not pertain to the
theologian properly, although he can and
should use them against those who deny the
mysteries of our faith, if these men will allow
no place for Scripture, Tradition, or the
definition of the Church. We should deal
with these people rather by human reason, so
as first to show the error of their belief, and
then, the probability of our own, especially
from its agreement with the true laws of
morality. These proofs do not pertain to
Theology: otherwise St. Thomas would not

have said that, against those who deny all the principles of 'Theology, there is nothing left for the theologian except to refute their arguments." *Ibid.*, art. 8, Dub. circa textum, n. 37. " The difficulties which are usually raised in this article seem to face not only the theologian, but also the logician; for the proper function of the latter is to provide the instruments or method for acquiring science and demonstration. Moreover, the logician treats *ex professo* of the nature and properties of science and of demonstration, which is the proper instrument for acquiring science. Indeed, this is the principal objective of the entire body of Logic, namely, to present the manner of constructing a demonstration. . . Therefore, to determine 'whether Theology is a science' belongs properly to the logician, who, when he knows the nature and the quality of the principles which the theologian assumes, i. e., how the theologian has arrived at a knowledge of them, and having examined the form of the syllogism whereby the theologian draws conclusions from those principles, can then easily decide whether Theology is properly a science and whether it uses the instruments of a true science." *Ibid.*, art. 8, Disp. IV, cap. i, n. 1.

"Lastly, Cajetan falsely asserts that this type of argument pertains to the theologian as such, in order to answer with positive evidence an objection whirls attacks a mystery, for the theologian does this only by acting as a philosopher. Nor are the principles of philosophy proper to Theology, except when they are employed with articles of faith to draw a conclusion. In this case the theologian takes these principles from philosophy, because Theology is in a certain sense subalternated to philosophy. . . But when the theologian argues from principles which are proper to philosophy only, as in the refutation of the aforesaid objections, he functions, not as a theologian, but as a philosopher. This must be so, because the theologian as such, cannot, from positive evidence (*evidenter positive*) answer any objection." *Ibid.*, art. 8, Disp. XI, cap. III, n. 6.

13.

3 *Summa Theol.*, q. I, art 6. In his *Commentary on the Sentences*, St. Thomas has this to say: "Whereas the speculative habits are, according to the Philosopher, three in number, namely, wisdom, science, and understanding, we maintain that (Theology) is Wisdom, from the fact that it considers the highest causes, and stands as the head, the rule, and the *ordainer* of all the other sciences. Indeed Theology is more worthy to be called wisdom than is Metaphysics, because the former considers the highest causes in themselves and as such, under inspiration received immediately from God. . . . But wisdom, as the Philosopher says in VI Ethics, considers both conclusions and

principles; hence wisdom is both science and an understanding, since science is concerned with conclusions and understanding with principles. , . . It must be said further that, just as the habit of first principles is not acquired through other sciences, but is possessed from nature, while the habit of conclusions deduced from first principles (is acquired), so also, in the doctrine (which is Theology) the habit of faith, which is like a habit of principles, is not acquired, although we do acquire the habit (a) of those things which are deduced from these principles (Theology's function as science); (b) of those truths which serve for their defence (Theology's function as wisdom)." *In I Sent.*, q. l Prolog. art. 3, sol. L, corp.; and sol. 2 ad 3.

14.
Summa Theol., I-II q. 57, art. 2, ad 1 and ad 2; q. 66, art. 5 ad 4.

15.
But nevertheless, reason guided by faith expands to the extent that it may penetrate more deeply the objects of belief, so that, in a certain manner it arrives at an understanding of them." *In I Sent.*, q. I, Prolog. art 3, sol. 3.

16.
"When reason, enlightened by faith, seeks diligently, devoutly, and soberly, it obtains, as

a gift from God, a certain most fruitful understanding of mysteries, both from the analogy of things which it knows naturally, as well as from the connection of the mysteries themselves with each other and with man's ultimate end." Denzinger, Enehiridion Symbolorura, 1796.

17.

From what has been said we can perceive what must follow. . . . Secondly, that Theology, as regards the understanding of Sacred Scripture, of the Councils and of other definitions, whereby what is of faith is declared immediately revealed by God, ought to be called the understanding of principles, and not science. If the true literal sense be evidently attained, then that faith is secured which is the certain, although not evident, principle of Theology. If, however, only a probable judgment is reached concerning the true sense (of a passage), then a merely probable principle will be had." *Commentaria* in I, q. I, art. 2, Disp. I (ed. Concha, 1852) , col. 24-c.

18.

Cfr. Ramirez, O.P., *De Hominis Beatitudine*, Tom. I. p. 4, note 5.

19.

Cfr. P. Voste, O.P., "*S. Thomas Aquinas*

Epistularum S. Pauli Interpres," in *Angelicum*"
(1942) , I, n. I, pp. 258-261

20.
I. q. I, art. 8, n. VIII.

21.
Summa Theol., I, q. 1, a. 3, ad 2.

22.
Ibid., q. 14, art. 16.

23.
Ibid., II-II, q. 4, a. 9, ad 3.

24.
Ibid., I, q. I, art. 5, ad 2.

25.
I Contra Gent., c. 1.

26.
Vatican Council, cf. Denzingcr, Enchiridion
Syntholorum, 1796.

27.
Catejan, I, q. 1, a. 8, n. IV.

28.
Summa Theol., I, q. 1, a. 4.

29.

"The virtues are principles in man of doing good in a human mode, according to the rule of human reason; the gifts, on the other hand, are impelling (*impulsiva*) principles, if I may so speak, inspiring the performance of good in a manner which is in a certain sense superhuman and divine. Consequently, when a man is moved by divine inspiration, he does not seem to be a mere man nor to experience a human inspiration, but one that is truly divine. . . In this lies the principal distinction between the gifts and the virtues, namely, that the virtues perfect man in a human manner, and according to the rule of human reason; whereas the gifts perfect man in a manner which is manifestly heroic and divine, and so they may be called divine virtues." Medina, I-II, q. 68, a. 8.

30.

Cfr. Ramirez, O.P., "De Ipsa Philosophia in Universum, Secundam Doctrinam Aristotelico-Thomisticam," in *La Ciencia Tentista*, XXVI (1922) , pp. 40-41.

31.

In I Sent., q. I, Prolog. a. I; *Summa Theol.*, I, q. 1, a. 5, ad 2; *In Boet. De Trinitate*, q. 2, a. 3, ad 7.

32.
Aristotle, *I Meta.*, *In I Meta.* lect. 2, n. 41-42; *Summa Theol.*, I, q. I, a. 6; I-II, q. 57, a. 2, ad I and ad 2; q. 66, a. 5, corp. and ad 4; *In Boet. De Trinitate*, Q. 2, a.3, ad 7.

33.
In I Sent., q. I, Prol. a. 3, sol. I; I, q. I, a. 6.

34.
Summa Theol., I, q. 1, a. 6.

35.
Ibid., ad 2.

36.
In I Sent, q. I, Prol., a. I.

37.
Ibid.

38.
Catejan, I, q. I, a. 8, n. VIII.

39.
De Potentate Civili, Prol.

40.
De Locis Theologicis, XII, c. 2, n. 4.

41.

Historia Eclesiastica, I, iv, p. liii

42.

The Manuscripts of Master Francis de Vitoria," by Fr. Beltran de Heredia, O.P., in *La Ciencia Tomista*, XXXVI (1927) , p. 67.

43.

De Locis Theologicis, II, c. 10, n. 4.

44.

Commentaria in I Partem D. Thomae, Prologus.

45.

In Boet. De Trinitate, q. 2, a. 1.

www.ingramcontent.com/pod-product-compliance
Lightning Source LLC
Chambersburg PA
CBHW072047040426
42447CB00012BB/3059